Homemade P
Kids Cooking Series

Some recipes included in this book were contributed from our Kids Cooking Activities readers.

About the Author

Debbie Madson is a Web Publisher and Author for children. She has several learning kids websites including:

www.kids-cooking-activities.com
www.kids-sewing-projects.com
www.teaching-money-skills.com

As well as teaching products to aid in these subjects through her websites and TeachersPayTeachers store.

http://www.teacherspayteachers.com/Store/Debbie-Madson

She has many Kindle ebooks for kids fun and entertainment. Debbie also has three kids who are great for helping and contributing to her projects.

Disclaimer and Terms of Use: Effort has been made to ensure that the information in this book is accurate and complete, however, the author and the publisher do not warrant the accuracy of the information, text and graphics contained within the book due to the rapidly changing nature of science, research, known and unknown facts and internet. The Author and the publisher do not hold any responsibility for errors, omissions or contrary interpretation of the subject matter herein. This book is presented solely for motivational and informational purposes only.

Introduction

Welcome to one of our cookbooks in our " Cooking with Kids Series"

If you have visited my website before http://www.kids-cooking-activities.com you'll know I'm a big believer in teaching kids to cook. Our slogan is **helping kids learn and grow up in the kitchen** and that is just what I'm hoping this series will interest you and your kids in doing.

Kids that learn to cook and help out in the kitchen are more likely to eat what they had a hand in creating. Which means that they will be interested in trying new foods and it is a perfect opportunity to teach them new healthier options.

You can involve your kids in cooking no matter the age. We have ideas on age appropriate tasks on our site here:

http://www.kids-cooking-activities.com/kids-cooking-lessons.html

But here in this cookbook I want to share with you some fun variations on Ramen noodle recipes to get you started. There are several sections including Salads, Soups, Main Dishes and some unique ideas. We tried to include a wide range of recipes that can interest many different taste buds so I hope you find quite a few recipes that your family will enjoy.

Some tips in cooking with your kids:

- Read the recipes, ingredient lists and cooking process fully before starting
- Set out all the cooking tools
- Start with a clean workspace and stove
- Always use fresh ingredients
- Always wash your hands before cooking
- What takes an adult a short amount of time may take your child longer so be prepared

Remember to supervise your kids while they are cooking in the kitchen.

All the recipes in this Popsicle cookbook are simple and do not need a stove or microwave. You can include your kids in the creating process and they will learn the names of different fruits, learn how to measure, and gain experience in working in the kitchen.

This cookbook covers 50 simple and tasty Popsicle recipes that are made from natural and homemade ingredients. Before starting the Popsicle making process, please note the following, it will help you in each recipe.

Basic Tools Needed:
Blender
Popsicle Molds
Hand mixer
Ice cream Wooden Sticks, if needed

Unmolding your popsicles

Take a bowl full of lukewarm water. Place the bottom of the popsicle molds in water for 20 seconds and pull the Popsicle out holding onto the stick.

Using different molds

We give the directions in the recipes often to semi-freeze molds for several hours and put the wooden ice cream sticks in the middle. Then freeze longer. You can add the stick from the beginning and then freeze but sometimes your stick may float to the side. Using plastic molds work great when the bottoms snap onto the mold.

Another idea if you don't have popsicle molds is to use paper cups with wooden sticks. Freeze and peel off paper when you are ready to eat.

Table of Contents

Popsicle Recipes

Orange Pop

Ingredients

2 fresh oranges

1/2 cup water

1/4 cup Jelly (Flavor of your choice)

Method

Take two fresh oranges and squeeze their juice in a bowl. Remove seeds and add half cup of water. Add jelly and stir well. Pour the mixture into molds. Snap tops of molds on and freeze. If using wooden ice cream stick, semi-freeze it for about 2 hours and put the wooden ice cream stick in the middle. Now freeze it for 6 hours.

(Serving for three)

Multi Layer Fruit Pops

2 Cups sliced fresh strawberries
3/4 Cup sugar, divided
1 1/3 Cups fresh peaches, sliced
2 cups diced watermelon
Puree in blender strawberries and 1/4 cup sugar.
Pour small amount in molds or paper cups about 1/3
full. Put in Popsicle sticks. Freeze.

Puree peaches and 1/4 cup sugar in blender. Pour
over frozen strawberry layer. Freeze. Cube
watermelon and remove seeds. Puree watermelon
and 1/4 cup sugar in blender. Pour over frozen peach
layer and freeze.

Pomegranate Pop

Ingredients

1 cup pomegranate seeds
2 tablespoons sugar
1 teaspoon vanilla essence

Method

Peel the pomegranate and blend the seeds in a blender. Place a piece of cheesecloth over a bowl or use a sieve with very small holes. Pour the juice in the bowl. Mix sugar and vanilla with the pomegranate juice. Pour the mixture into molds. Snap tops of molds on and freeze. If using wooden ice cream stick, semi-freeze for about 3 hours and put the wooden ice cream stick in the middle. Put back in freezer and freeze overnight.
(Serving for two)

~If you don't want to go to the trouble of peeling and seeding pomegranates replace with pomegranate juice.

Apple Pop

Ingredients

1 cup apple chunks

1 tablespoon honey

1/4 Cup milk

Method

Peel the apples and cut them into chunks. Pour all ingredients in the blender and blend until smooth. Pour the mixture into molds. Snap tops of molds on and freeze. If using wooden ice cream stick, semi-freeze for about half an hour and put the wooden ice cream stick in the middle. Now freeze it for 3 hours. (Serving for two)

Fruity Popsicle

2 liter lemonade, Sprite or 7 Up
sliced strawberries, kiwis, mangos, blueberries
Cut up slices of kiwi, fresh strawberries, mango or
other fruits you like and place in popsicle molds. Pour
lemonade or 7-up over the fruit. Add popsicle sticks
and freeze.

Peach Pop

Ingredients

1/2 Cup peach chunks
2 tablespoons sugar
1/4 tablespoon lemon
1/2 cup water

Method

Peel the peaches, remove pits and cut into chunks. Pour all the ingredients into a blender and blend until smooth. Pour the mixture into molds Snap tops of molds on and freeze. If using wooden ice cream stick, semi-freeze for about 1 hour and put the wooden ice cream stick in the middle. Now freeze it for 5 hours. (Serving for two)

Strawberry Pop

Ingredients

3 cups strawberries

1 cup milk

2 tablespoons sugar

Method

Pour all the ingredients in a blender and blend until smooth. Now pour the mixture in a bowl lined with cheese cloth or a fine strainer. Pour the juice into molds. This helps get rid of strawberry seeds. Snap tops of molds on and freeze. If using wooden ice cream stick, semi-freeze for about 2 hours and put the wooden ice cream stick in the middle. Now freeze it for 3 hours.

(Serving for eight)

Grapes Pops

Ingredients

1 cup fresh grapes
2 tablespoons sugar
1/2 tablespoon lemon juice

Method

Wash the grapes thoroughly. Add all ingredients in the blender and blend until smooth. Pour the mixture into molds. Snap tops of molds on and freeze. If using wooden ice cream stick, semi-freeze it for about a half hour and put the wooden ice cream stick in the middle. Now freeze it for 3 hours.

(Serving for two)

Orange Creamsicles

Ingredients

4 fresh oranges
1 cup vanilla ice cream
1/2 cup fresh cream
1 1/2 tablespoon sugar

Method

Take four fresh oranges and squeeze the juice in a
bowl. Remove seeds and whisk sugar into juice. Stir
until the sugar dissolves. Pour vanilla ice cream in the
bowl and continue to mix until it's smooth. Pour the
mixture into molds but fill only 3/4 part of the mold.
In a clean bowl, pour fresh cream and blend with a
hand mixer until smooth. Pour cream in the top part
of each mold. Snap tops of molds on and freeze. If
using wooden ice cream stick, semi-freeze for about
2 hours and put the wooden ice cream stick in the
middle. Now freeze it for 4 hours.
(Serving for eight)

Peachy Creamsicles

Ingredients
1/2 cup cubed peaches
1 tablespoon sugar
3 tablespoon water
1/2 tablespoon honey
2 tablespoon cream

Method
Pour all ingredients in a blender and blend until smooth. Pour the mixture into molds. Snap tops of molds on and freeze. If using wooden ice cream stick, semi-freeze for about a half hour and put the wooden ice cream stick in the middle. Now freeze it for 2 hours.
(Serving for one)

Whipped Creamsicles

Ingredients

1 Cup whipped cream
4 tablespoons vanilla extract
4 tablespoon orange extract
1 tablespoon cocoa powder
1/3 cup powdered sugar

Method

Take whipped cream in a bowl and blend with hand mixer until fluffy. Add vanilla and orange extract. Stir until smooth and add in powdered sugar.
Add cocoa powder. Pour the mixture into molds. Snap tops of molds on and freeze. If using wooden ice cream stick, semi-freeze for about 6-7 hours and put the wooden ice cream stick in the middle. Now freeze it for 24 hours.
(Serving for one)

Sweet Corn Creamsicles

Ingredients

2 cups sweet corn

1 cup cream

1/2 teaspoon vanilla extract

1 tablespoon sugar

Method

Pour all the ingredients in the blender. Blend until smooth. Pour the mixture into molds. Snap tops of molds on and freeze. If using wooden ice cream stick, semi-freeze for about 9 hours and put the wooden ice cream stick in the middle. Now freeze it for18 hours. (Serving for five)

Mango Pops

Ingredients

3 cups mango chunks
1 cup water
1 tablespoon sugar
1/2 teaspoon vanilla extract

Method

Pour all the ingredients in the blender and blend until smooth. Pour the mixture into molds. Snap tops of molds on and freeze. If using wooden ice cream stick, semi-freeze for about 3 hours and put the wooden ice cream stick in the middle. Now freeze it for 24 hours. (Serving for six)

Cookies Creamsicles

Ingredients

3 cup cookies, Oreo is our favorite

1 cup cream

1 cup milk

Method

Pour all the ingredients in the blender and blend well. Pour the mixture into molds. Snap tops of molds on and freeze. If using wooden ice cream stick, semi-freeze for about 3 hours and put the wooden ice cream stick in the middle. Now freeze it for 3 hours. (Serving for four)

Strawberry Cream Popsicle
by Brianne (California)

1 cup of strawberry nectar
1/2 Cup strawberries
1/4 Cup whipped cream

Beat mixture in blender, pour into molds and freeze.
Enjoy!

Peach-sicle

by Carmen

Put mandarin oranges or peach slices into the bottom of a plastic cup. Pour peach or orange juice into the cup until almost full. Poke a stick through a square of tin foil and into cup. freeze overnight. to get Popsicle out, run warm water on the outside of cup and gently slide Popsicle out.

Enjoy a healthy treat.

JELL-O-Creamy Pudding Pops

Ingredients

1 cup milk

1 cup Jell-O creamy pudding

1/2 cup whipped cream

Method

Pour whipped cream in a bowl and beat with hand mixer until fluffy. Add pudding mix and milk. Continue to beat until smooth. Pour the mixture into molds. Snap tops of molds on and freeze. If using wooden ice cream stick, semi-freeze it for about 2 1/2 hours and put the wooden ice cream stick in the middle. Now freeze it for4 hours.

(Serving for four)

Chocolate Truffle Cookie Pop

Ingredients

1 cup milk

2 cups crushed cookies or Nilla wafers

1 cup cream

1/2 tablespoon sugar

1 cup melted chocolate

Method

Pour the milk in a microwave bowl and heat until starts to boil. Add sugar, chocolate and cream and stir well.

Let the mixture cool. Pour mixture into blender and add crushed cookies. Blend well until smooth. Pour the mixture into molds. Snap tops of molds on and freeze. If using wooden ice cream stick, semi-freeze for about 2 ½ hours and put the wooden ice cream stick in the middle. Now freeze it for 4 hours.

(Serving for eight)

Fruity Pops

Ingredients
1/2 cup sliced strawberries
1 cup milk
1 tablespoon sugar
1 teaspoon vanilla extract

Method
Pour all the ingredients into a blender and blend well until smooth. Pour the mixture into molds. Snap tops of molds on and freeze. If using wooden ice cream stick, semi-freeze for about 1 ½ hours and put the wooden ice cream stick in the middle. Now freeze it for 8 hours.
(Serving for four)

Sparkling Blue Velvet Pops

Ingredients

1 cup blueberries

1 1/2 cup whipped cream

1/2 cup water

2 teaspoons cocoa powder

3 teaspoons royal blue paste food color

1/2 teaspoon violet paste food color

Method

Beat whipped cream until fluffy with hand mixer. Pour all ingredients in the blender. Pour the mixture into molds. Snap tops of molds on and freeze. If using wooden ice cream stick, semi-freeze for about 1 hour and put the wooden ice cream stick in the middle. Now freeze it for 6 hours.

(Serving for six)

~If desired, leave out food coloring

Oreo Pudding Pops

Ingredients

3 cups Oreo cookies, chopped

1 cup melted chocolate

1 cup prepared vanilla or chocolate pudding

Method

Melt chocolate in a microwave safe bowl. Add chopped Oreo cookies to the chocolate. Half fill the mold with chocolate Oreo mixture. Then pour cream pudding in the rest of the mold. Snap tops of molds on and freeze. If using wooden ice cream stick, semi-freeze for about 5 hours and put the wooden ice cream stick in the middle. Now freeze it for 10 hours.

Banana Pops

Half a banana
Chocolate chips or peanut butter
1 popsicle or wooden ice cream stick
Crushed nuts, chopped candies or topping of choice

Place chocolate chips or peanut butter into a
microwave-safe bowl and heat for about 20 seconds.
Use potholders to remove the bowl.
Peel the banana and slice it in half.
Place the stick into the cut end of the banana to make
a handle.
Spoon chocolate or peanut butter over the banana,
top with nuts, granola, or any other toppings and
freeze or chill for one hour.

Grahams Cream Pop

Ingredients
10 crushed honey grahams
1/2 Cup whipped cream
5 tablespoons honey

Method
Pour whipped cream in a bowl and beat until fluffy.
Add crushed graham crackers and honey to cream
and stir the mixture. Pour the mixture into molds.
Snap tops of molds on and freeze. If using wooden
ice cream stick, semi-freeze for about 2 ½ hours and
put the wooden ice cream stick in the middle. Now
freeze it for4 hours.
(Serving for two)

Red Velvet Pudding Pop

Ingredients

1 cup cherries

1 1/2 cup whipped cream

1/2 cup water

3 teaspoons red paste food color

Method

Beat whipped cream and pour all the ingredients in the blender. Pour the mixture into molds. Snap tops of molds on and freeze. If using wooden ice cream stick, semi-freeze for about 3 hours and put the wooden ice cream stick in the middle. Now freeze it for 6 hours. (Serving for four)

~Leave out red food coloring if desired.

Raspberry Coconut Ice Pop

Ingredients

1 cup sliced banana

1 cup coconut milk

1 cup raspberries

Method

Pour a cup of sliced bananas and milk into blender and blend well until smooth. Pour into molds, adding chunks of raspberries in layers. Snap tops of molds on and freeze. If using wooden ice cream stick, semi-freeze t for about 2 hours and put the wooden ice cream stick in the middle. Now freeze it for 5 hours. Makes 4 popsicles in large molds or about 8 in small paper cups.

Tomato Ice Pops

Ingredients

1 cup tomato juice
1/2 cup crushed ice
1 tablespoon sugar

Method

Mix the sugar into tomato juice and add in crushed ice. Pour into molds. Snap tops of molds on and freeze. If using wooden ice cream stick, semi-freeze for about 4 hours and put the wooden ice cream stick in the middle. Now freeze it for 7 hours.
(Serving for three)

Fruity Lemonade Pops

Ingredients

1 cup sliced mango
1/2 cup lemon juice
1/2 cup orange juice
1 tablespoon sugar

Method

Pour all the ingredients in the blender and blend well. Pour the mixture into molds. Snap tops of molds on and freeze. If using wooden ice cream stick, semi-freeze for about 5hours and put the wooden ice cream stick in the middle. Now freeze it for 10 hours. (Serving for three)

Strawberry Ice Pops

Ingredients

1 cup strawberries

1 cup crushed ice

2 tablespoons sugar

Method

Pour all the ingredients into a blender. Blend well until smooth. Pour the mixture into molds. Snap tops of molds on and freeze. If using wooden ice cream stick, semi-freeze for about 3 hours and put the wooden ice cream stick in the middle. Now freeze it for 6 hours. (Serving for one)

Cherry Pop

Ingredients

1 1/2 cups cherries

4 teaspoons sugar

2 tablespoons milk

2 cups of crushed ice

1/2 teaspoon salt

Method

Remove the pits of cherries and put all the ingredients in a blender. Blend well until smooth. Pour mixture into molds Snap tops of molds on and freeze. If using wooden ice cream stick, semi-freeze for about 2 hours and put the wooden ice cream stick in the middle. Now freeze it for 8 hours.

(Serving for one)

Peanut Butter Oreo Ice Pop

Ingredients

1 cup butter, softened
1 cup crushed ice
1/2 cup Oreos
1/2 cup peanuts

Method

Beat the butter until smooth. Add all other ingredients into butter. Pour the mixture into molds. Snap tops of molds on and freeze. If using wooden ice cream stick, semi-freeze for about 1 ½ hours and put the wooden ice cream stick in the middle. Now freeze it for 3 hours.

(Serving for four)

Soda Ice Pop

Ingredients

1 cup orange soda, lemon lime or whichever you like

Method

Pour the drink into molds. Snap tops of molds on and freeze. If using wooden ice cream stick, semi-freeze for about 1 ½ hours and put the wooden ice cream stick in the middle. Now freeze it for 1 ½ hours. (Serving for one)

Watermelon Ice Pop

Ingredients

2 cups watermelon

1/3 cup orange juice

1/3 cups water

Method

Blend all the ingredients. Pour the mixture into molds. Snap tops of molds on and freeze. If using wooden ice cream stick, semi-freeze for about 5 hours and put the wooden ice cream stick in the middle. Now freeze it for 7 hours.

(Serving for five)

Coconut Pineapple Ice Pop

Ingredients

1/4 cup coconut milk

1/2 cup pineapple juice

1 cup pineapple chunks

Method

Blend all the ingredients together in a blender until smooth. Pour the mixture into molds. Snap tops of molds on and freeze. If using wooden ice cream stick, semi-freeze about 5 hours and put the wooden ice cream stick in the middle. Now freeze it for 7 hours. (Serving for two)

Coco Nutty Pop

Ingredients

1 cup coconut milk

1/4 cup cashew

1/4 cup pistachio

Method

Blend all the ingredients in blender until smooth. Pour the mixture into molds. Snap tops of molds on and freeze. If using wooden ice cream stick, semi-freeze for about 5 hours and put the wooden ice cream stick in the middle. Now freeze it for 5 hours.

(Serving for two)

Blueberries Swirl Popsicle

Ingredients

1 cup blueberries

1 Cup blueberry yogurt

1 cup vanilla yogurt

Method

Add vanilla and blueberry yogurt into popsicle molds adding each one a little at a time creating layers. Add a few blueberries within the layers as well. Freeze

Hibiscus Pomegranate Pop

Ingredients

1 cup water

1 cup pomegranate juice

2 tea bags hibiscus

Method

Boil a cup of water and place 2 tea bags of hibiscus in it for 2 minutes. Add pomegranate juice in it. Pour into molds and freeze.

Papaya Pop

Ingredients

1 cup cubed papaya
1 tablespoon sugar
1 tablespoon honey
1/2 tablespoon lemon juice
1/2 teaspoon salt

Method

Blend papaya until smooth. Add remaining ingredients and blend together. Pour the mixture into molds. Snap tops of molds on and freeze. If using wooden ice cream stick, semi-freeze for about 2 hours and put the wooden ice cream stick in the middle. Now freeze it for 5 hours.
(Serving for two)

Watermelon Raspberry Lime Pop

Ingredients

1 cup watermelon

1/2 cup raspberries

1 cup lime juice

1/2 cup sugar

Method

Blend all the ingredients together. Pour the mixture into molds. Snap tops of molds on and freeze. If using wooden ice cream stick, semi-freeze for about 3 hours and put the wooden ice cream stick in the middle. Now freeze it for 5 hours.

(Serving for four)

Strawberry Lemonade Pop

Ingredients

1 cup strawberries

1/2 cup lemon juice

Method

Blend strawberries and lemon juice together until blended. Pour the mixture into molds. Snap tops of molds on and freeze. If using wooden ice cream stick, semi-freeze for about 5 hours and put the wooden ice cream stick in the middle. Now freeze it for 5 hours. (Serving for two)

Juice pops
by Megan & Isaac (IN)

We don't use exact amounts.
Orange Juice (probably 1-2 cups depending on how
many pops you are making)
Frozen or fresh fruit of choice (berries and bananas) -
cut up fruit as necessary to fit into blender
Puree all in the blender. Pour into popsicle molds.
Freeze. enjoy

Pear Pops
by Shakira (On)

Mix the following in the blender:
2 fresh pears
1 1/4 cup milk
1/4 cup sugar
Make sure the ingredients are smooth. Pour mixture into paper cups evenly. Place in freezer so contents do not pour out. After 20-30 minutes or until top layer is frozen stick a popsicle stick in the middle all the way to the bottom of the cup.
Freeze for another 2 hours and then peel pops out of the cups and enjoy!

Apple Swirl Popsicles

by michael

apple juice

apples

Cut apples and mix with juice. Pour in paper cup and put Popsicle stick in. Freeze.

Red Fruit Pop's

by Amy J.K. (Victoria BC)

1 cup raspberry yogurt

1/2 cup frozen raspberries

1 cup strawberry kiwi juice

Stir and pour into molds or cups and freeze.

Tropical Fruit Popsicles

1 Cup mandarin oranges with juice
1 Cup crushed pineapple
1 mango, chopped
2 Cups orange, pineapple or grape juice
Add ingredients to a blender and blend until smooth.
Pour into Popsicle molds and freeze.

Simple Juice Pops

Try mixing two juices together for a different flavor.
1 cup orange juice
1 Cup white grape juice
Stir together and pour into molds. Freeze.

Watermelon Popsicles

2 cups watermelon cubed remove seeds
1 cup apple juice
Blend in blender until smooth. Pour into Popsicle
molds and freeze.

Lemon Raspberry yogurt Ice Pop

Ingredients

1 cup lemon juice

1 cup raspberries

1 cup yogurt

Method

Pour lemon juice and yogurt in a bowl and add chunks of raspberries. Pour the mixture into molds. Snap tops of molds on and freeze. If using wooden ice cream stick, semi-freeze for about 2 hours and put the wooden ice cream stick in the middle. Now freeze it for 8 hours.

(Serving for eight)

Pineapple Popsicle recipe

1 quart milk
20 oz can of crushed pineapple, drained
1 1/2 Cups sugar
1 teaspoon vanilla
Blend in blender until smooth. Pour into molds and freeze

Tropical Popsicle

Makes 18 pops
2 cups lemonade
4 passion fruit, halved
1 large mango, peeled, chopped
1/2 pineapple, peeled, cored, chopped

Place the mango and pineapple in a blender or a food processor and blend until smooth.
Transfer the juice to a pitcher.
Add lemonade and passion fruit; stir to combine.
Pour the juice into the mold, secure with lids or insert paddle pop sticks and freeze until set.
Remove the pops from molds and enjoy!

Jell-O Pops

1 small package flavor gelatin
1 cup boiling water
1 cup vanilla or flavored yogurt
1/2 cup milk
Dissolve gelatin in boiling water. Allow to cool. Then stir in yogurt and milk Pour into Popsicle molds or cups insert sticks and freeze.

Made in the USA
San Bernardino, CA
08 April 2015